THE 5 MASCULINE INSTINCTS

Study Guide

CHASE REPLOGLE

CONTENTS

Introduction

CLIMBING
THE MOUNTAIN

"It is not what he has, or even what he does which expresses the worth of a man, but what he is."

HENRI-FRÉDÉRIC AMIEL

Climbing Mount Everest is hard. The physical demands are overwhelming. It is, perhaps, the ultimate test of physical endurance; the grueling climb and diminishing oxygen starves the body of life with each ascending step. Climbers are at the mercy of extreme weather patterns and exposed to some of nature's harshest conditions. The process of altitude acclimation and the ascent can take months, with complicated travel logistics requiring even more time. Procuring the proper paperwork, equipment, and guide fees cost tens of thousands of dollars. And all of this assumes you reach Summit's base camp physically and emotionally prepared for the actual climb. Still, every year, a few hundred men and women manage to make it to the summit.

On occasion, disaster strikes. In 2019, eleven people died attempting the climb, many of their bodies remain frozen on the mountain's slopes.[1] Experts claimed the high level of deaths was not due to avalanches, wind, or weather conditions, but to overcrowding and inexperience. "Some climbers did not even know how to put on a pair of crampons, clip-on spikes that increase traction on ice," guides later explained.[2]

Yet in 2021, Nepal issued a record number of climbing permits. Each year's disasters only seem to add to the mountain's allure and beckon another year's worth of climbers ready to risk their own lives and empty their bank accounts in pursuit of the world's highest achievement.

Surprisingly, most are not professionals. The catalog of Everest's climbers list their occupations as engineers, relators, airline pilots, attorneys, doctors, and students. Each goes hoping for that moment of standing on top of the world, and for that photo to prove they conquered it. Some write books about it, some work it into their motivational talks, but all, I imagine, keep that costly photo on the most prominent of their office shelves. Proof they have done what so few are capable of.

Everest has a secret though. While the photos capture their smiles—the red marks of their oxygen masks still pressed into their faces, clad in their bright down feather North Face suits, lifting their nation's flags or tokens from home—just out a frame are a group of men who seldom appear in the photos. They are the Sherpas.

* * *

In May of 2021, a new record was set on Everest. In addition to the record number of permits issued, a single climber reached the mountain's summit for his twenty-fifth time. In doing so, he broke his own record set the year before. In 2019, he climbed the mountain twice in the same year. Most recognize their summit of Everest as a once in a lifetime feat. By comparison he's done it more times than I've been to Disney, many more times. His name is Kami Rita Sherpa.

Kami is an Everest guide, a native of Nepal who makes his living leading his paying customers to the top. Prior to his occupation as a guide, Kami spent time in a monastery preparing to become a monk. He eventually took a job on the mountain as a base camp cook. When asked about his occupation, Kami once explained, "We were illiterate and poor and there were no other means of survival. As a result, we were compelled to climb dangerous mountains to eke out a living."[3]

Scientists have long marveled at the physical strength and endurance of the Sherpas. Many can work and climb with no oxygen and with far less rest than Western climbers require. Their bodies have adapted to life at extreme altitude.

Every year, hundreds of Sherpa workers climb Everest. They are there to prepare the mountain and guide its climbers. They fix lines and ladders to aid their client's ascent. They set up tents, haul stockpiles of oxygen to each of the camps, organize travel, keep a watchful eye on the weather, and provide lifesaving intervention for those who are injured or become ill. They serve as muscle, mentors, coaches, first responders, instructors, and sometimes counselors. They are the real climbers of Everest, not tourist, but the blue-collar working men of the mountain. They know how to put on a pair of crampons.

Kami is one of them, one of the best of them. He is not a millionaire, like so many of the men he leads. He is not sponsored by luxury outdoor brands. He started climbing Everest to feed his family and to ensure they had an education that kept them off the dangerous slopes.

In an interview with the BBC, he explained, "The Sherpas make their way, fixing the ropes, and the foreigners give interviews saying

Everest is easier. Or they talk about their courage, but they forget the contribution of the Sherpa." [4] Isn't life like that? Too often the camera cuts a man right out of the frame and with him the real truth of that moment and place. The camera supposedly loves a star, but it's rarely the star who knows what he's doing. He's usually an actor. As Tolkien put it, "All that is gold does not glitter." Sometimes the real thing is the thing most easily overlooked.

* * *

Man's attempts to prove himself by scaling mountains is just the beginning of the list. Most of us look for some sort of photo to put on the shelf. We look for some way to demonstrate we've done something worth capturing. Unfortunately, too much of masculinity has become about these outward displays. Like strutting male peacocks, we find our masculine niche and project it to the world, shifting our array of feathers to ensure the full image is always on display. We try to perpetually hold the pose and not give away the truth that we're smaller than we look.

Perhaps it is natural, perhaps even biological, but it still has consequences. Manhood becomes external. It becomes the professional domain of celebrities, and personalities, and those who flourish in the limelight. It becomes put on and obsessively defended. We post our selfie at the top of the mountain and hope to prove to others and ourselves that we've done it. We are real men.

The truth is most of us are tourists. We may convince others, but we know the truth somewhere deep inside. We know the feeling of the imposture. We're too often pretending. The problem is, we've located manhood in the wrong place, thinking it's something which must be affirmed by others.

True masculinity, though, is not something that can be shown off. It isn't a photo on Instagram, a trophy on a shelf, or a toy you rev to impress friends. The real work is less noticed. Less valued. And real men worry far less about having to prove it.

The men I know and respect most aren't flaunting it. They aren't out to prove anything to others or themselves. They aren't bragging about their achievements or posting them for the world to see. They are busy at their work. Fixing lines to the mountain's slope, laying down ladders to bridge icy ravines, setting up tents, cooking meals, packing bags with gear, and somewhere in the process setting records that usually go unnoticed. They are men not by what they do but by who they have become in the process.

I've always liked how the novelist John Steinbeck put it, "We value virtue but do not discuss it. The honest bookkeeper, the faithful wife, the earnest scholar get little of our attention compared to the embezzler, the tramp, the cheat."[5]

Perhaps manhood is always like that; in its best form it is always at risk of being overlooked. It is hard to see because, at its best, it doesn't care about drawing attention to its self. It is not hard to notice when it is wrong, anemic and destructive, or indulgent and gaudy. The real thing isn't desperate for any recognition. So it goes overlooked. Busy with its work, experience and character accumulating with each passing day, it becomes more valuable and less the center of the story.

My proposition is simple: There are men who only want to convince you that they are a men, hoping to also convince themselves by doing so. They're in it for the photo and they get a lot of the attention. But there are men who can lead us up the mountain. They are not necessarily influencers, athletes, politicians, podcasters, or celebrities, but they know their way around dangerous slopes. They can show us the way. They have fixed ropes for us to follow, marked our maps, and left provisions where they know we would need them.

The 5 Masculine Instincts offers glimpses into their lives: Cain, Samson, Moses, David, and Abraham. Not heroes but companions. Not men by their bravado, but by their failures and humble faith to press on. We are not trying to be them, but by following, we learn their lessons and a better instinct, a better character.

I realize that turning to the Bible to talk about masculinity feels cliché. Perhaps it feels too old-fashioned. But there is something in things old which seem now forgotten. There are paths to virtue which seem too long lost. I think it's worth looking to those now too often overlooked. Those who have reached the summit before us.

No one climbs the mountain alone. We do it together, we do it with a guide. Perhaps one day, with time and experience, we become experts ourselves, but for now, we are humble enough to know we have plenty still to learn.

Find some men, or perhaps just a single friend, and let's see where these Biblical companions might lead us.

"When I was climbing, I built up a close relationship with the Sherpa people." SIR EDMUND HILLARY (first man to reach the summit of Everest with his Sherpa partner, Tenzing Norgay)

GETTING STARTED

"It is an ironic habit of human beings to run faster when we
have lost our way."
ROLLO MAY

You need a plan. Character doesn't develop by chance. It takes an effort of intentionality to accomplish anything. The plan doesn't have to be complicated or costly, but if you're going to get the most out of *The 5 Masculine Instincts* and this study guide, a simple plan will help you do it.

A plan will also help you follow through with the commitment you've making to this book and study. It's easy to get yourself excited about a new possibility, about growing in character, clarifying what it means to be a man, and intentionally maturing in Christlikeness. But don't be surprised how quickly that excitement can wane. It does so partly because we get distracted and allow our commitments to fall away. But you can also lose momentum due to the difficulty of the work. Introspection is hard. Vulnerability is so often avoided. While this guide won't ask you to pour your heart out in some group circle-session, if you're unwilling to be honest with at least yourself and God, you won't make much progress.

* * *

The Apostle John saw an angel descending from heaven. It was not some soft, feathery figure with a harp. The angel's face shone like the sun. Wrapped in a great cloud, his legs descended to earth like fiery pillars, with one foot planted on the sea, the other on land. Opening his mouth, he spoke like a roaring lion. John described his voice as an army of seven hundred men. Eagerly, John prepared to write down the words of this angelic messenger. Such figures do not speak triviality; John meant to catch every word.

But a heavenly voice interrupted him and told him to put down his pen. Instead, he was instructed, "Go, take the scroll that lies open in the hand of the angel who is standing on the sea and on the land." As John approached, he saw it—a small scroll laid open across the angel's hand. Asking for it, the angel gave John a very strange command. "Take it and eat it. It will turn your stomach sour, but in your mouth, it will be as sweet as honey." John ate the scroll.

> "But sooner or later we find that not everything is to our liking in this book. It starts out sweet to our taste; and then we find it doesn't sit well with us at all, it becomes bitter in our stomachs. Finding ourselves in this book is most pleasant, flattering even, and then we find that the book is not written to flatter us, but to involve us in a reality, God's reality, that doesn't cater to our fantasies of ourselves." — Eugene Peterson, *Eat This Book: A Conversation in the Art of Spiritual Reading*

The work God is doing in you often feels like that. The possibility is sweet, but digestion takes time and often forces us to recognize things uncomfortable and disconcerting. You will not become a better man if every time you experience pain you turn away. Somethings you must face soberly to grow beyond them. And so it will be if you really hope to get something out of this book as well. Stick with it, even when it's hard, even when it's sour.

USING THIS STUDY GUIDE

This study guide follows the chapters in *The 5 Masculine Instincts*. There are nine chapters in the book and nine sessions in this guide. I recommend that you read each chapter and complete the corresponding study guide session before moving on to the next. Each session draws from the stories and Biblical examples found in the book. Your pace depends on who you are completing this study with; however, a chapter per week is a good goal.

PERSONAL REFLECTION

For each session, you will find an:

1. Introduction
2. Questions for personal reflection
3. Group discussion questions
4. Prompts for prayer
5. Next steps

Work through the introduction and personal reflection sections on your own. These reflection questions will be more personal than the group questions. They will help you reflect on your own life and instincts. You won't be expected to share these answers in a group setting but taking the time to do personal reflection will help enrich your later discussions on the topic.

GROUP DISCUSSION

I highly recommend you find someone to read the book with and discuss what you're learning. Just as the book depends on the lives of other men to help us learn, so too we grow better when we are discussing the challenges we face with other men.

In its simplest form, your group discussion could be a single friend you join regularly for coffee or lunch. After each of you have read a chapter and completed the personal reflections, take time to discuss what you've learned. You can use the group discussion questions as prompts for even casual conversations.

This study guide is designed primarily for a small group setting. Each man should have a copy of *The 5 masculine Instincts* and this study guide. Remind the men in your group that there is an audio book version of *The 5 Masculine Instincts*. Audio books are a great way to read and preferred by many men.

A chapter per week fits the pace of most small groups. This would provide a nine-week series, around two months. You'll find the list of questions in the group discussion sections long enough for a meaningful conversation. Consider adding your own or choosing the questions most appropriate for your group.

You might also consider using this book for a men's retreat. Ask participants to come having read the book and completed the personal reflection sessions. If nine sessions are too many for your retreat, consider covering only the five instinct chapters. The additional sessions could be completed through casual conversations or independently.

TIME FOR PRAYER

The lessons in this book need time to sink in. Prayer is the best tool for humbling yourself and allowing the Spirit to work the gospel into your life. At the end of each session, I've included several prompts for prayer. Feel free to use these in your group session and personally. There are enough to use throughout the week as well.

Through prayer, God will guide you, convict you, encourage you, and give you strength. The danger of this endeavor is imagining that you can do it alone, that you can make yourself a better man on your own. At best, you feed pride and at worst become disillusioned by the whole project. Prayer allows you to combine your desire to grow with the humble reality of your need for God's help in doing it. If this study guide accomplishes nothing more than to move you to frequent and honest prayer, it will prove life changing.

NEXT STEPS

Each session concludes with a next steps section, an objective task you can work on implementing throughout the week. These next steps are a great way to continue thinking about and applying each chapter.

***

How ever you choose to use this study guide, create a plan and stick to it. Think hard and pray honestly. It's worth it. You won't stumble your way into becoming a better man. Your instincts won't mature naturally into Christlikeness. Be honest about yourself and think deeply about the gospel. By this you will mature and grow in character.

My prayer is that *The 5 Masculine Instincts* and this study guide will draw you closer to God. That it will inspire you to believe in a better manhood, one formed by His goodness and grace. This study guide is a tool, to help you follow the men of the Bible as they lead each of us to a deeper relationship with God. He is our aim, our destination, our goal, our reward—our source for a better manhood.

ADDITIONAL RESOURCES

Visit the5masculineinstincts.com/downloads/ for additional personal and group resources including:

- Session videos
- Podcast episodes
- YouVersion reading plans
- Sharable graphics

"The books or the music in which we thought the beauty was located will betray us if we trust to them; it was not in them, it only came through them, and what came through them was longing. These things—the beauty, the memory of our own past—are good images of what we really desire; but if they are mistaken for the thing itself they turn into dumb idols, breaking the hearts of their worshipers. For they are not the thing itself; they are only the scent of a flower we have not found, the echo of a tune we have not heard, news from a country we have never yet visited."

C. S. LEWIS, *The Weight of Glory*

SESSION 1

MASCULINE MALAISE

CHAPTER 1: MEN, MEAT, AND THE MASCULINE MALAISE

"Every characteristic absence of spirituality, every piece of
common vulgarity, is due to an inability to resist a stimulus—
you have to react, you follow every impulse."

NIETZSCHE

INTRODUCTION

In the opening chapter of *The 5 Masculine Instincts*, I describe the current situation many men experience as malaise. Perhaps that's a new word for you, but I'm guessing the feeling is not. I like how the Oxford dictionary defines it

> **ma·laise:** /məˈlāz/ (noun)
> a general feeling of being ill, unhappy or not satisfied, or that something is wrong in society, without being able to explain or identify what is wrong.

Malaise is exactly what I think many men are feeling. Something is wrong. Something isn't working. But we can't quite put our finger on it. Why is it confusing to be a man today? Why do we feel on the defensive even when we're not sure what we're defending?

I'm often struck by how difficult it is to give a definition of manhood, or more particularly a definition of what it is to be a Christian man. Do you have a good working definition of manhood?

Most of the men I know want to be better, want to grow and mature into a better manhood, but few seem sure of how to go about it. We settle into this malaise, this vague sense of unease, not sure what to do about it. I write in *The 5 Masculine Instincts*:

> I've long been haunted by a line in one of Walker Percy's novels. "Men are dead, dead, dead; and the malaise has settled like a fall-out and what people really fear is not that the bomb will fall but that the bomb will not fall . . . I know nothing and there is nothing to do but fall prey to desire."
>
> We become nothing more than what we feel. We become our instincts. Some can articulate it; they can talk about this experience of moral discouragement and disillusionment. Others express it only through their disengagement, too often coping through substance abuse, escaping through fantasy, pornography, and video games or vicariously living through the success of sports teams and politicians.
>
> So many are caught in this malaise. An uneasiness, a weariness, an unshakable sense that so much is wrong, that nothing really matters, and nothing can really be done about it anyway. Longing for something meaningful while simultaneously laughing at those who believe in such things. We give up on getting better, settling into this malaise as just the way we are as men. Indulging our raw instincts and question-

ing anyone who would question us, everything seemingly hostile. We're not sure what else to do with what we feel, afraid to admit we feel at all. We defend what we never really chose. We pick fights to avoid ourselves. Make enemies to have something worth fighting for. All of it an indulgence in this instinctive unease. What else is there to guide us?

In what is perhaps the most dangerous mistake of all, we come to think that mindless indulgence in our instincts is the proof of our masculinity, that what we feel must be our deepest truth; to risk any kind of introspection, a threat to manhood itself. We come to think that this male malaise is masculinity. To indulge is masculine. To question your instincts is only to take the bait and jeopardize the whole game.

The question we must all come to terms with is how do we become better men today, in this complicated and controversial world? We can't allow ourselves to give up on the possibility. We can't indulge what we don't understand? We have to seek out better advice on how to be better men.

PERSONAL REFLECTION

Take some time to read through the first chapter of *The 5 Masculine Instincts* then work through the questions below. These are meant for personal reflection. You won't be asked to share them, so be as honest as you can.

1. For the past few years, there has been an ongoing cultural conversation about masculinity. Much of it has centered around the idea of toxic masculinity and an indulgent alternative. How is our culture's critique of masculinity impacting you?

2. Some think the church has contributed to toxic masculinity. I think it's more of a mixed bag. Many churches have struggled to respond to the cultural questions in a compelling way. How has your church experience impacted the way you think about masculinity and manhood?

3. Have you experienced the unease and malaise I described in the first chapter?

4. How can this malaise and the unending controversy around masculinity lead us to "fall prey to desire?" What are the consequences?

_____

_____

_____

_____

_____

5. In *The Philosophy of the Unconscious*, Eduard von Hartmann defines an instinct as "a purposive action without consciousness of the purpose." We do things for a purpose but are unconscious of why. Instincts lead us to act even when we have not fully decided how to act. How aware are you of the instincts at work in your life?

_____

_____

_____

_____

6. Why are instincts so difficult to recognize?

_____

_____

_____

_____

7. In *The 5 Masculine Instincts,* I raise C. S. Lewis's question, that the real dilemma of our instincts is deciding which should be trusted and which should be checked. Not all instincts are bad, but if left unconsidered they have a tendency to lead us toward destruction. How are

our instincts different from sin? How can they lead you to sin?

_____

_____

_____

_____

8. Nietzsche suggested that we force our instincts to rationalize themselves. We should test our instincts to determine why we feel them and if they are helpful. How might you force your instincts to rationalize themselves? What might you discover?

_____

_____

_____

_____

GROUP DISCUSSION

"I'm convinced this is the challenge costing too many men a better manhood. In a world of individualized truth and hyper-defensiveness, we've lost the ability to decide what to do with our instincts. We have failed to become their master. Instead, they rule us." (*The 5 Masculine Instincts*)

I open *The 5 Masculine Instincts* by discussing the controversy around men eating meat. It seems we can't even agree on a man's proper diet. If a steak is that controversial, what else is confusing about being a man today? In the first chapter, I tried to capture the current challenges facing our pursuit of manhood. Those challenges are not just from one side. Some call masculinity toxic while others indulge every impulse assuming that the raw instinct is somehow the only path to be a man. What gets left out is the all-important conversations about how men actually develop character and become better.

1. Have you experienced the confusion and controversy of talking about masculinity today? Have you experienced the malaise I described in the chapter and in the previous personal reflection section?

2. It's easy for us to allow our position on the topic of masculinity to become our sense of manhood. We can think that a particular theological position or argument is enough to make us a man. How is the controversy and debate around masculinity robbing us of becoming better men?

3. I mention in the book that the two cultural approaches to mas-

culine instincts are to consider them toxic or salvific. How have you seen these two approaches in the world around you?

_____

_____

_____

_____

4. Neither of these approaches deals with our deeper instincts? How do our instincts rule us?

_____

_____

_____

_____

5. Why is it difficult for us to recognize our own instincts?

_____

_____

_____

_____

6. What are the consequences of trusting our instincts? Why should we learn to rule them?

_____

_____

....

....

....

7. How might your life change if you began to recognize your instincts and master them?

....

....

....

....

PRAYER PROMPTS

Below are some ways that you can pray as a group or individually between sessions.

- *God, protect my heart from discouragement and malaise. Even when I'm challenged, let me not act out of defensiveness or bitterness but allow me to consider how you might want me to grow.*

- *God, give me the courage to take a closer look at my own motives and instincts. Teach me to see where they have mastered me. Show me where I too often indulge and trust my instincts alone.*

- *God, give me a new hunger to become a better man. Help me not to give up. Help me sense that it is still possible and that you're willing to help show me the way.*

NEXT STEPS

The next steps offer suggestions for how to apply these ideas to your life. What are some intentional steps you could take this week to make this session more than just reflections and discussion?

- Try to recognize a moment of impulse when you felt compelled to act in a particular way. Ask yourself the question, should that instinct be checked or trusted? We are going to learn more about what instincts to watch out for, but this simple step of beginning to recognize and question your instincts is a huge step forward in the process.

Session 2

THE 5 INSTINCTS

CHAPTER 2: LEARNING TO RECOGNIZE YOUR INSTINCTS

"Telling us to obey instinct is like telling us to obey 'people.' People say different things: so do instincts. Our instincts are at war."

C. S. LEWIS

INTRODUCTION

As a pastor, I recognized quickly that people act out of very different motivations. The same sins can be motivated by very different impulses. Making things more complicated, we often fail to recognize the instincts which motivate our actions. To us, they all seem like common sense. How can you objectively recognize something you feel so strongly?

The 5 Masculine Instincts originally began as a book on Samson. I noticed a tendency in young men, myself included, to become restless with life. Desperate for adventure, plenty of writers and marketers have used that restless need for adventure as a hook to sell their books and market their products. It isn't that adventure is sinful, not at all, but if unchecked and undiscerningly indulged, it has a tendency to weaken commitment and produce even greater restlessness. Adventure rarely produces contentment.; it leaves us hungry for more.

As I began to work on the book, I noticed how that restlessness often leads to a form of apathy and disengagement. It can also lead to a desperate attempt to portray a reputation and a fierce determination to protect it. What I discovered is that there are multiple instincts driving men to act. The real problem men are facing is their struggle to know what to do with those instincts.

Around that same time, I came across Shakespeare's stages of a man. Shakespeare did not invent that idea. For generations, philosophers and writers have recognized that men tend to act out of common instincts. As far back as Ovid, there have been listings of similar stages and impulses. Recognizing these instincts helped me push the conversation deeper. It's not enough to talk about the external temptations of money, sex, and power, we need to explore deeper to the instincts which make those things seem disproportionately important. It's the instincts that lead a man to act, to take, to fear, and to go.

Learning to recognize your instincts opens a door to mastering them instead of being mastered by them. Recognizing your instincts is the gateway to growing beyond them, what previous generations of men have called character, the maturing and checking of instincts in acquisition of something more useful.

I soon discovered that we are not alone in this work. Far from being our models of perfected masculinity, the men of the Bible are our companions. As the author of Hebrews put it, we are surrounded by a great cloud of witnesses. Men who knew the same instincts, who both failed by them and, by faith, also overcame them toward something better.

I concluded in the book:

> The goal of this book is not to annihilate your masculine instincts or to pull them back to some safer middle ground. The goal is to help you recognize the proper counterbalances necessary to keep those instincts from leading you into collapse. What you need is enough self-knowledge to recognize your instinct and a counterweight—an intentional practice of faith—by which to balance it and experience the power of His grace. You need the work of developing character to help you steward the ship and see it safely to its final port. The men of the Bible are your companions for doing just that.

PERSONAL REFLECTION

As a part of this session's personal reflection, I recommend you take a few minutes to complete the Masculine Instincts Profile Assessment. The assessment includes 25 questions to help determine your instinct profile. You can take the assessment online for free. You can visit the5masculineinstincts.com/profile or use the QR code on this page.

A word on taking the assessment, try to answer quickly and honestly. Don't over think the questions. The results page will show you how your instincts breakdown across the 5 masculine instincts. It's important to remember that this assessment is not conclusive or absolute. It is a tool to get you thinking about your instincts. We are all a mix of instincts, and there are certainly more impulses than the five I've included in this book. But the assessment will help you start evaluating your instincts and, as we discussed before, force them to rationalize themselves.

1. What were your percentages across the five instincts?

Sarcasm: ....

Adventure: ....

Ambition: ....

Reputation: ....

Apathy: ....

Review the descriptions of each instinct found in chapter 2 of *The Five Masculine Instincts*. You can also find them online: the5masculineinstincts.com/instincts

2. After rereading the descriptions of your top instincts, do you see evidence of them at work in your life? Consider writing down a few examples.

....

....

....

....

....

3. Do you recognize the other instincts in men you know, perhaps your father, son, or close friends?

4. How could these instinct be impacting who you are as a man?

GROUP DISCUSSION

C. S. Lewis described two critical questions for making moral progress: do we know how to coordinate our movements among others and are our ships in good enough condition to carry out those maneuvers? Our culture pays a lot of attention to how men act within society but very little attention to how men learn to maintain their own vessels. Learning to recognize your instincts helps you begin to understand the ship you're guiding. Recognizing your instincts helps you plan out the required maintenance and pay closer attention to the particular characteristics of your vessel. That is critical work for keeping the ship in order.

The Apostle Paul instructed Timothy to watch his life and doctrine closely. Paul was giving Timothy advice for maintaining his vessel. It would require self-knowledge and gospel-knowledge. That is how we move forward as men. And the Bible gives us a long list of men to help us learn to do it. Through their failures and success, we learn to recognize our own instincts. And by the grace of God at work in their lives we come to recognize the gospel's power in our own.

1. After reading chapter 2 of *The 5 Masculine Instincts*, do you recognize any ways you've been miss reading the men of the Bible?

2. What does it mean to see these Biblical men as companions not heroes?

3. What do you take away from C. S. Lewis's concern that we've neglected the work of maintaining seaworthy vessels, an analogy for the neglect of our instincts and character formation?

4. What are the consequences of this neglected work?

5. Why is knowing yourself not enough to become a better man?

6. What else is needed?

7. I'm often struck by how little we talk about character, and even less about how character is formed. Why have we neglected the work of discussing and developing character?

8. How do the men of the Bible and their witness to the gospel's power lead us to a better manhood?

PRAYER PROMPTS

Below are some ways that you can pray as a group or individually between sessions.

- *God, thank you for the lives of the men in the Bible. Thank you for the way you walked with them through failures and short-comings so that I might recognize the way you are gracious and faithful to me as well.*

- *God, help me to better understand myself. Don't allow me to blindly indulge my instincts but show me why I act the way I do and show me where I need to grow and change.*

- *God, help me to recognize all of the resources you have given me in the Gospel. Grow my hunger for your word and for a deeper understanding of your grace and mercy.*

NEXT STEPS

The next steps offer suggestions for how to apply these ideas to your life. What are some intentional steps you could take this week to make this session more than just reflections and discussion?

- Make sure you have completed the profile assessment. Over the next few days, pay attention to your actions. Can you recognize your top instincts at work in motivating your actions and thoughts? Take some notes on how those instincts showed themselves.

Session 3

SARCASM

CHAPTER 3: SARCASM: THE HUMOR OF OUR AGE

"The arrows of sarcasm are barbed with contempt."

WASHINGTON GLADDEN

INTRODUCTION

We all enjoy a good joke, and these days, few jokes are more popular than one with sarcastic. I make clear in *The 5 Masculine Instincts* that sarcasm is not a sin. I don't intend to imply that a good man will have forever denounced the sarcastic quip, hardly. But like so many things in life, things are not always what they appear. That is the particular danger of sarcasm. It appears funny on the surface but it is often thin cover for contempt.

One of my favorite dictionaries defines sarcasm as, "a satirical remark uttered with some degree of scorn or contempt; a taunt; a cutting jest."[8] What all definitions of sarcasm share are a sense of hostility beneath the joke. We use sarcasm in contempt, to taunt, to cut. When the sarcastic eye is rolled at authority, it is usually not difficult to recognize it as a rebellion. So it is that Cain scorned the authority of God, sarcastically biting back, "Am I my brother's keeper?" Sarcasm is the first instinct we will look at.

In Shakespeare's categorization, it is associated with the young schoolboy. Though it comes first in our list, it's important to note that it is not limited to the young. Sarcasm is often a symptom of a disinterest in learning, maturing, or submitting. To be sure, this is a hallmark of adolescent hubris, but so too of the disillusioned or bitter man. It is a lack of humility, a defiance of character, and a lack of respect that lets loose the sarcastic tongue.

> **SARCASM:**
> The first instinct is the boy, dressed for school but dragging his feet, whining and reluctant to take on the responsibility of learning the ways of the world. He is not just young by age, but by his immaturity and his unwillingness to grow up. His jokes and antics are a cover for contempt. He is quick to complain, convinced the world is unfair, and desperate to avoid the burden of knowing. Instead, he lives by what he feels. His sarcasm is an instinct which leaves him vulnerable to his own ignorance.

In many ways, this instinct comes first simply because, without the humility to receive God's divine lesson and correction, we stand little chance of cultivating true character. The muscle must be stressed to strengthen. The blade must be filed to become sharp. And the man must be offended before he can undertake the work of true virtue.

* * *

If sarcasm is a concealed form of contempt than its proper check requires humility. Humility is a Christian sounding word, familiar and easily affirmed, but I'm struck by how difficult it can be to define and how few have a plan for pursing it. I suggest the Christian virtue of meekness as a starting point.

PERSONAL REFLECTION

Take some time to read through the third chapter of *The 5 Masculine Instincts* then work through the questions below.

1. Do you consider yourself to be a sarcastic person? Do others see you as sarcastic?

2. How might moments of sarcasm in your life hint at rebelliousness or contempt? How might you be using humor to hide it?

3. I write in *The 5 Masculine Instincts* that our culture makes us experts at criticizing problems, but often lacks the wisdom to improve them. How are we taught to prioritize criticism?

4. How is taking responsibility key to maturing and developing character? How well do you take on responsibility?

5. What is your definition of humility?

6. How did this chapter challenge your concept of meekness?

7. I like to think of meekness as an inner strength which doesn't need to prove itself. How much are your actions really reactions and how well can you control your impulse to react?

GROUP DISCUSSION

"A sarcastic person has a superiority complex that can be cured only by the honesty of humility."

LAWRENCE G. LOVASIK

Cain's story is only a few sentences, but it is a profoundly important turning point in the Biblical story. It is through Cain's struggle that sin is first mentioned. The rejection of Cain's sacrifice left him bitter and conspiring. God warned, "sin is crouching at the door. Its desire is contrary to you, but you must rule over it."

Preachers and commentators have long speculated on why God rejected Cain's sacrifice, but that may not be the right question. We don't know why Cain's sacrifice was rejected because he never asked. Cain revealed instead his contempt for God's authority and his unwillingness to be challenged or taught. His sarcastic retort, "Am I my brother's keeper?" exposed the lack of humility that would stunt his moral growth.

1. How could God's rejection of Cain's sacrifice have been an opportunity for Cain to learn more about God and himself?

2. What does God's warning that "sin is crouching at the door... you must rule over it" mean?

3. How is Cain sarcastic and what does it reveal about his character?

4. The title of this chapter in *The 5 Masculine Instincts* is, "The Humor of Our Age." Do you see signs of contempt in the sarcasm of our culture?

5. How is humility related to sarcasm and why is humility a starting point for growing in character?

6. Meekness is rarely identified as a character goal, but the ability to not react is a critical form of strength. We are only able to learn God's lessons if we are capable of pausing and reflecting where our instincts insist we respond. How did this chapter change the way you think about meekness?

7. How might humility and meekness have changed Cain's response to God?

8. How does the gospel help us grow in humility and true meekness?

PRAYER PROMPTS

Below are some ways that you can pray as a group or individually between sessions.

- *God, forgive me for my defensiveness and my unwillingness to be corrected. I realize your discipline is for my good. Help me receive your lessons with humility so that I might not be destroyed by the sin crouching at my door.*

- *God, I know I'm not always humble. Teach me how to be more self-suspicious. Make me hungry to learn and more willing to listen.*

- *God, Do not let me be mastered by sin or driven by instinct. Help me to cultivate the strength of meekness. Help me not to act out of reaction but to consider how you might be at work in better ways.*

NEXT STEPS

The next steps offer suggestions for how to apply these ideas to your life. What are some intentional steps you could take this week to make this session more than just reflections and discussion?

- This week, pay attention to your impulses to act, particularly to react to things that bother you or annoy you. Recognize the moment and choose to slow down your reaction, your words, perhaps even your rolled eyes. How difficult is it to not react? How might that moment be a lesson in how God is leading you to grow?

Session 4

ADVENTURE

CHAPTER 4: ADVENTURE: CULTIVATING NEW EYES

"The man who said, 'Blessed is he that expecteth nothing, for he shall not be disappointed,' put the eulogy quite inadequately and even falsely. The truth 'Blessed is he that expecteth nothing, for he shall be gloriously surprised.' The man who expects nothing sees redder roses than common men can see, and greener grass, and a more startling sun. Blessed is he that expecteth nothing, for he shall possess the cities and the mountains... Until we realize that things might not be we cannot realize that things are."

G K CHESTERTON

INTRODUCTION

Adventure is one of humanities most compelling narratives. Our movies and novels all depend on it and most of us have spent plenty of time day dreaming about adventurous places we would love to be. Certainly there is nothing wrong with a little adventure; there's nothing sinful about an adrenaline rush, but our need for adventure as a means to prove ourselves and to define ourselves, has a tendency to cost us important things.

I've seen first hand how a restless need for adventure can cause a man to neglect and even sacrifice his marriage, family, career, and place. Perhaps what we have been calling adventure isn't an adventure at all. Can it be an adventure if you choose it, plan it, and put it on the calendar? Or are adventures better understood as something you find yourself in and accept through commitment?

Samson's story is a great place to wrestle with that question and this instinct. Samson found himself caught between two forces, the commitment of his Nazarite vows and his passion to explore, romance, and face-off with death. Samson's story helps us better understand the importance of discernment and how only through discernment and commitment can we truly understand the story we are in.

Shakespeare described it as a young man equally restless for new landscapes and the pursuit of love. I describe the instinct this way in *The 5 Masculine Instincts:*

ADVENTURE:

In the second of the stages, Shakespeare described man as a lover. He is driven by passion and idealism. His is the world of romance and quests. His instinct is to go, to travel off onto the horizon in search of his true identity, heroic exploit, and love. Shakespeare likened him to a sighing furnace, burning within and thwarted without. His instinct is for the pursuit of adventure.

I've always loved Proust's expression, "The real voyage of discovery consists not in seeking new landscapes but in having new eyes." That's what I hope Samson's story offers you too, new eyes to discover and recognize what God is doing in your life.

Ultimately, the goal of this chapter is not to steal your future adventures, its to help you discover better ones, deeper ones, ones which God by his sovereignty has already placed you in. It will take commitment. It will take time. It will take learning to quiet the restlessness of your instincts and instead recognizing more of the story unfolding around you. But, by God's grace, like Samson, you will discover it too. You'll discover that God's plans are not so easily lost.

PERSONAL REFLECTION

Take some time to read through the forth chapter of *The 5 Masculine Instincts* then work through the questions below.

1. How restless do you feel with your current life?

_____

_____

_____

_____

2. It is easy to become discontent and imagine that if your life was more adventurous it would have greater meaning. How much of your identity comes from pursuing remarkable experiences?

_____

_____

_____

_____

3. How did Samson's story resonate with your own?

4. How would you describe your ability to commit to things long-term, particularly things which may not always feel exciting?

5. Think about past times you've failed to keep a commitment. Are there discernible patterns in those failures?

6. Have your past broken commitments had negative consequences on you or the people you care about?

7. How might your struggles with commitment be keeping you from the better adventure God is offering you?

GROUP DISCUSSION

"Adventure is not outside man; it is within."

GEORGE ELIOT

Samson's story has often been misunderstood. At times, the Bible seems to present him as heroic, at other times, his life is sad and pitiable. Men have long struggled with what to make of him. But that maybe part of the point. Samson is like us, a mixed-bag of desires and consequences.

What we do learn from Samson's story is to wrestle with our own questions of adventure and identity. By his lack of discernment we are challenged to think more deeply about our own desires and about the experiences of our own lives. By God's grace, and by Samson's example, we can discover God's plans and a better adventure without the pain or destruction so central to Samson's life. Samson's story is an invitation to recognize in your life what he too often missed in his own.

1. Where do you see evidence of Samson's restlessness and what was it that kept motivating Samson to go down to the Philistine cities?

_____

_____

_____

_____

2. What did Samson's need for adventure cost him? How did it impact the divine calling on his life?

_____

_____

_____

_____

3. Why is commitment important?

_____

_____

_____

_____

4. How does commitment allow us to recognize and discern deeper things in our lives?

5. How is commitment related to maturity and the development of Christian character?

6. What was it that finally allowed Samson to recognize God's plan for his life?

7. How does the gospel help us recognize a better adventure than we might choose for ourselves?

PRAYER PROMPTS

Below are some ways that you can pray as a group or individually between sessions.

- *God, forgive me for how often I have neglected your calling and broken my commitments to the things that matter most.*

- *God, I need your help to discern what you are doing in my life. Help me sense your calling and the value of the commitments you have placed before me.*

- *God, do not let me live in restlessness but instead commit more deeply to the people, place, and work in which you have placed me. Help me to grow in character as I commit more deeply to your leading.*

NEXT STEPS

The next steps offer suggestions for how to apply these ideas to your life. What are some intentional steps you could take this week to make this session more than just reflections and discussion?

- Commitment is something you must practice. You become

better at it as you learn to recognize its value and how to quite the restlessness of your instincts and desires. What is something you could make a new commitment to? It's best if it's something long-term and unrecognized. It should be something between you and God, not necessarily glamorous but meaningful.

Session 5

AMBITION

CHAPTER 5: AMBITION: A PROMISED LAND LOST

"Well is it known that ambition can creep as well as soar."

EDMUND BURKE

INTRODUCTION

Of the five instincts included in the book, perhaps no other instinct is more highly valued in our culture than ambition. There is no disputing the good that ambition has produced. From exploration to invention, our world has been shaped and aided by the ambitions of men. It's easy to recognize great ambition in the Bible as well. Paul made it his aim to preach Christ where no other man had, pretty ambitious. Most of us have some form of ambition. Ambition itself is not sinful, but we should be honest enough to admit that our ambition can quickly turn bad. Ambition for good can often quietly mutate into a dangerous and desperate form of pride.

Perhaps the most dangerous quality of ambition is its tendency to become fixated on an outcome, desperate in its drive, and without careful attention prone to outpace God. We begin to make demands of those around us and of God himself. We begin to feel the weight of the demands we place on ourselves as well. Ambition quickly leads to despair and even disillusionment. Here is how I think of ambition, both its value and risk.

> **AMBITION:**
> The third stage is the soldier's. His instinct is for oaths and honor. His vision of sacred purpose carries him onto battlefields and into the world's pressing conflicts. He believes he is capable of righting wrong. He is quick to quarrel and quick to make demands, always with an opinion and passionate belief. Believing he is destined for something great; he is prone to visions which cast his sight constantly into the future. His instinct is the pursuit of his ambition.

What ambition needs is a test, a test by which we can discern its desperation and keep it in its proper place. I think the best test of ambition is your ability to put it down. Can you turn it off? Can you stop?

If our culture obsesses over ambition, it is also uninterested in the discipline of rest. We are not a people prone to sabbath. It's telling that many now think of sabbath rest as a life-hack for gaining enhanced productivity on the other six days. Even our approach to rest is biased by our ambition to get things done. We have lost the real lesson and test of ambition that rest was meant to be.

Moses is a great place to learn about ambition. You may have thought about Moses as reluctant, not ambitious, but ambition is often like that. In one moment it can be wild and audacious and in the next discouraging and debilitating. Moses experienced the wild swings of ambition. He saw ambition at its best and worst. He can help us better understand our own ambitions and learn to check them with rest.

PERSONAL REFLECTION

Take some time to read through the fifth chapter of *The 5 Masculine Instincts* then work through the questions below.

1. How would you define ambition and how have you personally experienced it?

    _____

    _____

    _____

    _____

2. What are some of the ambitions, dreams, and goals that you have for life? It's okay to be honest. As we saw in this chapter, ambition is not sinful but we need honesty and a test to keep it in its proper place.

    _____

    _____

    _____

    _____

3. When we fail to realize our goals ambition often swings into dis-

illusionment. You can become jaded and bitter, frustrated by the very thing that once inspired you. How have your ambitions led you to frustration and disillusionment?

_____

_____

_____

_____

4. How can ambition lead us to stop trusting God? Have you experienced this tenancy?

_____

_____

_____

_____

5. How difficult is it for you to stop what your doing? Do you struggle to rest?

_____

_____

_____

_____

6. How do you practice sabbath? How have you struggled with sabbath?

_____

_____

_____

_____

_____

7. What might your struggles with sabbath and rest suggest about
    your ambitions and the danger it might pose?

_____

_____

_____

_____

GROUP DISCUSSION

"The proud person always wants to do the right thing, the great thing. But
because he wants to do it in his own strength, he is fighting not with man, but
with God."

SØREN KIERKEGAARD

Moses is remembered as one of the greatest leaders in Israel's history. He was the visionary who led Israel out of Egyptian slavery, through the wilderness years, and to the borders of the promised land, but Moses's leadership was a struggle. At times Moses's ambitions were remarkably clear and God-centered, but as his task wore on, he found himself frustrated, disillusioned, and faltering in faith.

Ultimately, Moses's frustrated ambitions would cost him the promised land. God did not allow him to finish the task and lead the people in. It is hard to read, harder still to imagine, but Moses seems to have accepted God's decision with a humble understanding. By so doing, he offers us a lesson in evaluating our own ambitions and recognizing the critical test of sabbath rest.

1. How did Moses struggle with ambition? Where do you see his ambition motivating his actions and where do you see it frustrating him?

_____

_____

_____

_____

2. How did Moses's frustrations and discouragement signal he was no longer trusting God but depending on his own action and ability?

_____

_____

_____

_____

3. Dietrich Bonhoeffer claimed that "God hates visionary dreaming." What did Bonhoeffer mean and how can our visions lead

us to judge one another and God?

4. How is sabbath a test of our ambitions?

5. Why is rest so hard for us, especially as men?

6. Is it possible to be ambitious in your work and also embrace a life style of sabbath rest? What might that look like?

7. How does the gospel equip us to rest and not be burdened by our own ambitions?

PRAYER PROMPTS

Below are some ways that you can pray as a group or individually between sessions.

- *God, forgive me for so often going my own way. I realize that my ambitions can lead me to ignore you and demand things which aren't in your good will.*

- *God, help me to recognize my ambitions before they make me desperate and before they make me disillusioned. Help me to be honest about what I want and why I want it so badly.*

- *God, teach me how to rest. Teach me to keep a sabbath. Let me learn to test my ambitions by setting them down. Help me to find a deeper rest in you, to trust you more with the things I desire most.*

NEXT STEPS

The next steps offer suggestions for how to apply these ideas to your life. What are some intentional steps you could take this week to make this session more than just reflections and discussion?

- Practice sabbath. Perhaps you are already practicing some form of sabbath worship. How can you use that day for deeper rest. Set aside a day each week to not work on your goals or objectives. Recognize that you are not as productive as you could be and entrust that time to God. But don't just pay attention to the clock, recognize your own emotions. How capable are you at stopping? Does rest cause you stress or anxiety?

Session 6

REPUTATION

CHAPTER 6: REPUTATION: THE IMAGE OF A KING

"Give a man a reputation as an early riser and he can sleep 'til noon."

MARK TWAIN

INTRODUCTION

It is hard not to think about your reputation, perhaps it's impossible. We care about how we are perceived and the things for which we are known. It takes a life time to earn a good reputation and naturally, that isn't something we easily sacrifice. A reputation is something we have earned, something we may even deserve. Our good name comes from a lifetime of hard work. We aren't wrong to honor those who have earned a reputation for character and virtue and we should be motivated to earn the respect of others and keep it.

But a reputation can never be defended at the expense of truth. When our reputation becomes more important than the honest integrity of our lives, it is no longer a good thing. A reputation becomes a facade, a disguise, a dangerous game prone to our collapse.

As men, we are notoriously known for the compartmentalization of our lives. We hope that with enough success in one public area, we can cover over the rest of the messier and less respectable parts. We construct our identities on what can be seen and work tirelessly not to expose anything private. This game comes to be expected. We neither expect the full truth from others nor ourselves. We play only the part we're expected to play. Here is how I explained it in the book:

REPUTATION:

By stage four, the man has found enough success and money to become interested in his reputation and comfort. Shakespeare even recognized that by this stage, he had usually begun to put on some extra weight—I'm not pointing any fingers. He learns to dress and properly cut his beard, now conforming to the expectations of society. He becomes who he is expected to be and determined to protect his hard-earned respectability. His instinct is to guard his reputation.

If you read the Biblical story of David and Saul, you will soon recognize how central is the question of reputation. Saul's rule was founded on his reputation for looking like a king, and in nearly every story, David's dependence on his reputation would be tested. David had an incredible reputation. He had defeated the giant Goliath, been anointed king by Samuel, and called a man after God's own heart. Slowly, David came to trust his reputation at the expense of integrity. He not only sinned but went to exceptional lengths to cover it up and protect his public reputation.

Eventually, the truth always finds its way out. It did in David's life and it does in ours as well. When the truth emerges, we are destroyed by it, or taught to embrace a deeper form of integrity. Let's take a look at the true meaning of integrity and how confession offers us a better way forward.

PERSONAL REFLECTION

Take some time to read through the sixth chapter of *The 5 Masculine Instincts* then work through the questions below.

1. We all rightfully consider our reputation and how best to maintain it but we should be honest enough to recognize that it can become too important. How important is your reputation to you?

2. What are the things you would like to be known for? Are there things about yourself you're trying to hide?

3. Do you tend to compartmentalize your life? Are there parts of your interior life you prefer to avoid thinking about or discussing?

_____

_____

_____

_____

4. Do you recognize any consequences from avoiding these parts of your life? Has it impacted your relationships, work, or faith?

_____

_____

_____

_____

5. In *The 5 Masculine Instincts*, integrity is defined as a life fully-inventoried; there are no unexamined parts. How would you evaluate the integrity of your life?

_____

_____

_____

_____

6. What has been your experience with confession? Is it a regular

part of your spiritual life?

7. Do you have any relationships in which you are fully known and to whom you can confess things you feel tempted to hide?

GROUP DISCUSSION

"The mind and flesh of man are set on fire by pride; for it is precisely in his wickedness that man wants to be as God. Confession in the presence of a brother is the profoundest kind of humiliation. It hurts, it cuts a man down, it is a dreadful blow to pride... In the deep mental and physical pain of humiliation before a brother—which means, before God—we experience the Cross of Jesus as our rescue and salvation. The old man dies, but it is God who has conquered him. Now we share in the resurrection of Christ and eternal life."

DIETRICH BONHOEFFER

No one struggled more with the integration of their public and private life than David. At times, he managed it with remarkable integrity. Still, even David, a man after God's own heart, found himself overcome with the temptation to hide behind his success.

Few other Biblical characters offer us such a profound warning about the consequences of a divided life. David's story pleads to us to embrace a better integrity. We do it for the sake of our own lives but also for those we care most about. Without integrity, even the most impressive structures are soon to collapse.

1. How is clothing symbolically important throughout David and Saul's stories? How is it related to our experience of reputation?

2. How can your reputation be both a beneficial goal and a dangerous temptation?

3. How would you define integrity? How did this chapter change how you think about integrity?

4. When did David get integrity right? What were the benefits?

5. When did David fail to live up to integrity? What were the consequences?

6. The Bible explicitly commands us to confess sins to one another, yet we often find that difficult to do, often ignoring the command altogether. Why is confession so difficult for us?

7. How does the message of the gospel empower us to embrace real integrity and does it give us the courage to practice true confession?

PRAYER PROMPTS

Below are some ways that you can pray as a group or individually between sessions.

- *God, forgive me for the parts of my life I have tried to cover up and hide from you. I realize that you know all things and my attempts to avoid parts of my life leave me vulnerable to collapse.*

- *God, give me the courage to look honestly at my own life and give me the courage to confess my sins to you and to other men you have placed into my life. Do not let me go on living in false integrity.*

- *God, teach me how to live a life of integrity and let me feel the freedom and joy of no longer carrying around my secrets. Let my life be transparent before you and know the power of your gospel and grace in every part of my life.*

NEXT STEPS

The next steps offer suggestions for how to apply these ideas to your life. What are some intentional steps you could take this week to make this session more than just reflections and discussion?

- Confession is hard but we have to do it. It's that simple. No one is asking you to put your sins on a billboard or share every detail with the whole world. But you do need someone to whom you can confess. Perhaps it is a close Christian friend, a pastor, or brother. Find someone and confess something. Build on that confession. Search your heart and life for things which need to be inventoried and confessed. Get started.

Session 7

APATHY

CHAPTER 7: APATHY: A WORLD TOO WIDE

"He did not care what the end would be, and in his lucid moments overvalued his indifference. The danger, when not seen, has the imperfect vagueness of human thought. The fear grows shadowy; and Imagination, the enemy of men, the father of all terrors, unstimulated, sinks to rest in the dullness of exhausted emotion."

JOSEPH CONRAD

INTRODUCTION

Shakespeare describes man's final stage before death with the phrase, "a world too wide." Most of us have felt it. We inevitably come to realize that the world is wide and far beyond our control. Life reveals the limits of our ability to control relationships, careers, and family. Build a house and immediately it will begin to deteriorate. Live in it long enough and the evidence is unavoidable. The maintenance is exhausting and the work is never done.

Sociologists have long pointed out how we tend to disengage as we age. It is particularly true for men. We become less socially involved, we have fewer friends, we participate in fewer activities, and, as some studies have suggested, may even laugh less. But this gradual detaching from society doesn't always come with age. Disillusionment, failure, and frustration have caused many men to settle into apathy and disengagement. Wherever men find the world too wide and too complex to engage, apathy soon sets in.

The 5 Masculine Instincts describes this fifth stage as:

APATHY:

By stage five, he has grown tired of all this work and complexity. The "world is too wide," as Shakespeare put it. With age, his voice has begun to fade; it is symbolic of his engagement with the world. His vision is dulled. He is most comfortable in his slippers and recliner. He doesn't venture out as much as he used to. Content with his hobbies and luxuries, he knocks around the house. The world is complex, and by his experience, the recognition of inadequacy and mortality cannot be ignored. His instinct is to protect his autonomy and to disengage from what he cannot control. His highest purpose is to be left alone. His instinct is for apathy.

Abraham understood the complexity of life. He spent most of his life following God to an unknown destination, a path marked with frustration, conflict, and loss. It's not hard to recognize how his lack of control left him feeling the same apathy. But God, by his grace, tests Abraham, forcing him out of his apathy and into the life of faith. God tested Abraham by asking him to sacrifice his son Isaac.

It is certainly one of the most difficult passages of scripture, but the consequences of disengagement can be just as devastating. Few things bring greater destruction, pain, and brokenness than the disengaged disinterest of men. God wouldn't allow Abraham to succumb to it. By his grace he won't let us either.

PERSONAL REFLECTION

Take some time to read through the seventh chapter of *The 5 Masculine Instincts* then work through the questions below.

1. How do you respond to the phrase, "a world too wide?" How have you experienced what Shakespeare was describing?

   _____

   _____

   _____

   _____

2. Have you ever felt disillusioned and apathetic about something you once cared deeply about? What were the consequences of your apathy?

   _____

   _____

   _____

   _____

3. It is common for culture to warn about the accesses of masculine aggression, but how can an excess of disengagement be equally destructive?

4. Have you witnessed apathy and disengagement in the lives of the men you know? How has it impacted you?

5. How do you respond to the idea of God testing Abraham and how can we learn to think of God's tests as a gift?

6. How does sacrificing keep our faith active and alive?

---

7. Are there particular things God might be asking you to sacrifice that your apathy might be causing you to protect?

GROUP DISCUSSION

"The worst sin toward our fellow creatures is not to hate them, but to be indifferent to them: that's the essence of inhumanity."

GEORGE BERNARD SHAW

God's command to prepare Isaac as a sacrifice is one of the most startling passages in all of the Bible. Generations of preachers and commentators have struggled to communicate both its horror and profound importance. Much could, and has, been said about it, but perhaps a good place to begin is recognizing how it moves Abraham out of his apathy and back into a world of faith.

Abraham's story seems to come to a natural conclusion. The

major crises of his life had all resolved, and it is perhaps at this moment Abraham was at greatest risk. It is so easy for our faith to atrophy and deteriorate in our comfort. God's test pulls Abraham back into active participation.

1. Why do men have a tendency to disengage from the things we can't control?

2. When do you see Abraham acting apathetically? What were the risks and consequences of his disengagement?

3. How can age contribute to apathy? How can apathy be experienced at any age?

4. How can our disappointments and failures lead us to apathy?

5. How does sacrifice test our constant need to be in control?

6. How did God's testing of Abraham reengage his faith?

6. What are the signs that our faith needs to be reengaged?

_____

_____

_____

7. How can we keep our faith engaged even when we feel over-whelmed, discouraged, or tired? How do we live with faith in a "world too wide?"

_____

_____

_____

_____

_____

PRAYER PROMPTS

Below are some ways that you can pray as a group or individually between sessions.

- *God, forgive me for neglecting the perseverance of faith. I recognize how my faith has sometimes diminished. I recognize how apathy has allowed me to disengage the life you have called me to live.*

- *God, by the power of your Spirit, awaken my faith out of apathy. Give me a new sense of your calling and purpose for my life. Do not let apathy become my guiding impulse.*

- *God, give me the courage to sacrifice the things which keep me from looking to you. Help me to sacrifice even my comfort for the sake of deepening faith.*

NEXT STEPS

The next steps offer suggestions for how to apply these ideas to your life. What are some intentional steps you could take this week to make this session more than just reflections and discussion?

- Take some time to consider the things you try to avoid in life. Are there things you avoid simply because you can not control them? What might God want you to sacrifice in order to trust him more? Often we protect our time, comfort, and possessions. Apathy becomes a way of justifying their indulgence. What time, comfort, or possession could you sacrifice as an act of worship in order to reengage your faith?

Session 8

MOVING FORWARD

CHAPTER 8: THE REAL WORK AHEAD

"Go forward? Only thing to do! On we go!" So up he got, and trotted along with his little sword held in front of him and one hand feeling the wall, and his heart all of a patter and a pitter."

J.R.R. TOLKIEN

INTRODUCTION

Every book is about something more than just its title or chapter outline. *The 5 Masculine Instincts* is not just about these five instincts. Perhaps none of them applied to you. Perhaps you think I've made too much of them. It's never been entirely about them. What the book is really about is developing the skills necessary to grow, mature, and cultivate character.

The introduction of *The 5 Masculine Instincts*, explained, "Our culture has become highly skilled in pointing out the problems, but, beyond public service campaigns and news head- lines, we haven't developed the same expertise in helping men solve those problems. We have lost the wisdom by which men become better, by which they mature into a better manhood." That is what the book is really about, rediscovering the wisdom by which men before us grew in Christian character.

In chapter eight, you read about the Apostle Paul's advice to the young man Timothy. Timothy was leading in a complex environment. The ancient city of Ephesus was awash with every possible religion and perspective. Even in the church, the men were caught in endless debates and conflict. As a young leader, Timothy was up against a lot. Paul gave him a simple piece of advice.

> "Be diligent in these matters; give yourself wholly to them, so that everyone may see your progress. Watch your life and doctrine closely. Persevere in them, because if you do, you will save both yourself and your hearers." (1 Timothy 4:15-16)

Timothy would make progress in his own life and in the congregations he led but focusing his attention on his life and on the gospel. This is how we move forward as men. And this is what *The 5 Masculine Instincts* has really been about, learning to watch your own life and the gospel more closely. That is how we too make progress as men.

The gospel possesses power. Apply it carefully to your deepest instincts and it can infuse a character and virtue in ways effort alone can't. Paul's advice is for us too. This is how we make progress.

PERSONAL REFLECTION

Take some time to read through the eighth chapter of *The 5 Masculine Instincts* then work through the questions below.

1. How would you evaluate your growth in character? How often do you think about character?

    _____

    _____

    _____

    _____

2. How is real manhood related to the development of character?

    _____

    _____

    _____

    _____

3. What are the things which keep you from growing in character?

    _____

    _____

    _____

    _____

    _____

4. What does Paul mean when he suggests Timothy watch his life more closely?

_____

_____

_____

_____

5. How would you evaluate your own self-knowledge? How could you pay closer attention to your life?

_____

_____

_____

_____

6. What did Paul mean by keeping a watch on the gospel?

_____

_____

_____

_____

7. How would you evaluate your knowledge of the gospel? How could you pay closer attention to it?

_____

GROUP DISCUSSION

"Fame is a vapor, popularity is an accident, riches take wings, those who cheer today may curse tomorrow and only one thing endures—character."

HARRY TRUMAN

Paul's hope was that Timothy's work to grow in self-knowledge and gospel-knowledge would not only impact his own life but also those he led. When we grow in character it's not just to our own benefit, we bear responsibility and serve others with greater results. What our culture, churches, and families need, are men growing in Christ-like character, men who can serve and lead with virtue, self-knowledge, and gospel clarity.

1. How has *The 5 Masculine Instincts* really been about growing in character?

----

2. How does learning to watch your life more closely contribute to developing character?

3. How does paying closer attention to the Gospel contribute to developing character?

4. How do these two disciplines work together? How does watching your life help you better understand the gospel and how does attention to the gospel help you better understand your life?

5. What is unique about the Christian approach to character?
    How is it different from how the world tries to improve?

_____

_____

_____

_____

6. Why is character a key component of what it means to be a
    better man?

_____

_____

_____

_____

PRAYER PROMPTS

Below are some ways that you can pray as a group or individually
between sessions.

- *God, help me to better understand myself. Help me to better understand my instincts and desires. Let my growing self-knowledge contribute to humility and to receiving your gospel in deeper ways.*

- *God, help me to better understand the gospel. Help me to understand what you have done for me. Help me to receive the power of your gospel into my life and let it infuse me with true virtue.*

- *God, help me to grow as a man by developing better character. Help me to serve others and bear greater responsibility as I grow in character. Let my growth in character glorify you.*

NEXT STEPS

The next steps offer suggestions for how to apply these ideas to your life. What are some intentional steps you could take this week to make this session more than just reflections and discussion?

- Ask yourself where you need to pay closer attention. Is it in self-knowledge or gospel-knowledge? These two works should progress together, but often we have neglected one of the two. Where might you need to place greater attention?

•

Session 9

NOTHING TO PROVE

CHAPTER 9: NOTHING LEFT TO PROVE

"I live before the audience of One—before others I have nothing to gain, nothing to lose, nothing to prove."

OS GUINNESS

INTRODUCTION

This study guide opened with the story of one of the greatest mountain climbers in history. Yet, few know his name, and my guess is, you probably don't remembered it either. Why would you? Kami Rita Sherpa climbs for a living. He climbs to feed his family and to clothe them. He's not a celebrity or an influencer.

Every year, hundreds of people climb Everest for all kinds of reasons, but many, if not most, do it to prove something. They climb to prove something to themselves and to others. We are like them, living to prove things. Our sense of manhood is often the same. We imagine that manhood is something that can be proved, something that needs to be proved. We try to prove our manhood to others and just as often to ourselves. But I'm not convinced it can be, nor should be proved. Manhood is the byproduct of an entirely different pursuit, a better one. Manhood is the byproduct of Christ-like character forming in our lives. Any attempt to prove ourselves men, quickly deteriorates into gimmicks and caricatures.

Most falls, you'll often find me in some Missouri field behind my bird dog Millie hunting quail. Anyone who has learned to wing shoot learns an important lesson about aiming. There are somethings you can't hit by aiming at them. Aim at them and you'll miss them altogether. The beginner has a bad habit of sticking the gun at the bird, aiming at the whole, usually throwing their gun up and pulling the trigger in a kind of ambush, the gun fixed at the spot where they had seen the bird. You always miss. To hit the bird you have to be in movement. You have to swing the gun and you have to aim in front of the bird. You don't aim at the bird you aim where he will be.

On a bird rising in front of you over a pointed dog, you'll have to lose sight of the bird as you blot him out behind the barrel. To hit him you have to lose him.

***

In the final chapter of *The 5 Masculine Instincts*, I used Jesus's parable of the barren fig true to make the same point. You can't force fruit to grow. Fruit is the byproduct of soil, water, sun, and time. The best you can do is fertilize the soil and wait. With patience and the sovereign gifts of rain and sun, fruit begins to bud and grow. You have done it, but you've not really done anything at all. Your work isn't amongst the limbs but hands in the dirt.

Manhood is not something you can prove, nor should you give

it so much of your attention. That's not where the real work resides. Manhood is something you discover to be there when you need it, a byproduct of more important work. Manhood is not a card you earn or a certificate you frame and hang behind your desk, carefully placed for visibility in all those video conference calls. Proving it is far less important than actually possessing it. Possessing it is less important than the work required for it to grow. You need an instinct of faith, the careful work of life and gospel. Spread that manure, give it some time and manhood will be there when you need it.

PERSONAL REFLECTION

Take some time to read through the ninth chapter of *The 5 Masculine Instincts* then work through the questions below.

1. What are some of the ways we feel the need to prove manhood? What have you been trying to prove?

_____

_____

_____

_____

_____

2. How do you know that you are a man?

_____

_____

_____

3. What should you be focusing on to become a better man?

4. What have you taken away from reading and studying *The 5 Masculine Instincts*?

GROUP DISCUSSION

"Greatness lies, not in being strong, but in the right using of strength; and strength is not used rightly when it serves only to carry a man above his fellows for his own solitary glory. He is the greatest whose strength carries up the most hearts by the attraction of his own."

HENRY WARD BEECHER

Jesus's parable of the barren fig tree seems to end without an ending. The gardener requested more time to spread more manure and wait. But we aren't told if it worked. We aren't told if figures appeared the next year, or even if the land owner agreed to the plan. It is a parable about the owner's instinct to move on and the gardener's instinct to wait and trust. Few things are more difficult than waiting, or working at it while we wait, but somethings only grow that way. Manhood and Christ-like character only grow like that.

1. How is growing in character like the gardener's work to care for the fig tree?

_____

_____

_____

_____

2. What is the work we should be doing to grow as men?

_____

_____

_____

_____

3. What are the risks of trying to prove your manhood to others and to yourself?

_____

_____

....

....

....

4. How is faith a better instinct that helps us grow as men?

....

....

....

....

5. What have you learned from *The 5 Masculine Instincts*?

....

....

....

....

6. How has the book impacted the way you think about masculinity and manhood?

....

....

....

....

PRAYER PROMPTS

Below are some ways that you can pray as a group or individually between sessions.

- *God, free me from the need to prove my manhood. Do not let me live desperate or insecure for others' approval or my own. Help me to care more about the real possession of it than the proof.*

- *God, give me patience to cultivate real character. Help me to focus on the right work and sustain that work over a life time. Help me to continually grow more like you.*

- *God, help me to realize that faith is the missing instinct I need. Let it become the dominant instinct of my life. Let me live and react out of this better instinct of faith. And let it shape me and grow me into a better man.*

NEXT STEPS

The next steps offer suggestions for how to apply these ideas to your life. What are some intentional steps you could take this week to make this session more than just reflections and discussion?

- What comes next? That's a question you should be asking yourself. It's time to take responsibility for your life and faith. God is speaking. He is willing to lead you in this work but it requires you humble yourself, listen, and follow. Where is the Spirit leading you to grow, to spread more manure, to give greater attention, to become a better man? That is a life-long question, but the question starts today?

ABOUT THE AUTHOR

Chase Replogle is the pastor of Bent Oak Church in Springfield, Missouri. He holds a degree in Biblical Studies and an M.A. in New Testament from The Assemblies of God Theological Seminary. He is currently a D.Min. student in The Sacred Art of Writing at Western Theological Seminary.

Chase's work draws from history, psychology, literature, and a rich narrative approach to Scripture to help readers think more deeply about faith and life.

He has written for Christianity Today, The Gospel Coalition, Ekstasis, Bible Engagement Project, and Influence Magazine. In addition, he hosts the Pastor Writer Podcast (pastorwriter.com), where he interviews Christian authors on writing and publishing. A native of the Ozark woods, he enjoys being outdoors with his wife and two kids, sailing, playing the guitar (badly), and quail hunting with his bird dog Millie.

ENDNOTES

1 Alexandra Svokos, "How one of the deadliest seasons on Mount Everest unfolded, leading to 11 deaths," *ABCNews*, May 29, 2019, https://abcnews. go.com/International/deadliest-season-mount-everest-unfolded-leading-11-deaths/story?id=63319438.

2 Kai Schultz, Jeffrey Gettleman, Mulib Mashai, and Bhadra Sharma, "'It Was Like a Zoo': Death on an Unruly, Overcrowded Everest," *The New York Times*, May 26, 2019, https://www.nytimes.com/2019/05/26/world/asia/mount-everest-deaths.html.

3 Sangam Prasai, "Everest climber Kami Rita returns to break his own world record," *Agencia EFE*, April, 19 2019, https://www.efe.com/efe/english/life/everest-climber-kami-rita-returns-to-break-his-own-world-record/50000263-3956381.

4 "Sherpa climbs Everest twice in a week, setting record 24 ascents," *BBC News*, May 21, 2019, https://www.bbc.com/news/world-asia-48346341.

5 John Steinbeck, *Travels with Charley: In Search of America*, (New York: Penguin Books, 1986), 183.